Shiba Training Book

How to Guide a Shiba Inu

Basics

___

The Basics

Chapter One

Having Fun While Training

Training your Shiba Inu can be an incredibly rewarding experience, both for you and your furry companion. One of the keys to successful training is making sure it's enjoyable for both you and your dog. In this chapter, we'll explore how to infuse fun into your training sessions, ensuring that your Shiba Inu looks forward to learning and growing with you.

The Importance of Fun

Before we dive into specific training techniques, it's essential to understand why having fun during training is crucial. Dogs, including Shiba Inus, are more likely to engage and learn when they enjoy the process. When training sessions are enjoyable, your Shiba Inu is more likely to be focused and motivated, making the training experience productive and memorable.

Incorporating Play

1. Interactive Toys: Utilize toys that are not only fun to play with but also serve as training tools. Toys like puzzle feeders, tug toys, and treat-dispensing toys can keep your Shiba Inu engaged while reinforcing desired behaviors.

2. Fetch: Shiba Inus generally love a good game of fetch. Use a ball or a frisbee to work on commands like "come" and "drop it." This not only reinforces obedience but also provides a great opportunity for exercise.

3. Hide and Seek: Hide and seek is a fantastic way to work on the "stay" and "find" commands. Have someone hold your Shiba Inu while you hide, then call them to come find you. When they do, reward them with treats and praise.

Incorporating Treats

1. Training Treats: Invest in some high-quality training treats that your Shiba Inu adores. These should be small and easy to chew so that training doesn't turn into mealtime.

2. Treasure Hunt: Create a mini treasure hunt by hiding treats around the house or in your backyard. Encourage your Shiba Inu to use their nose to find the hidden goodies. This taps into their natural hunting instincts and is a fun mental exercise.

3. Obstacle Course: Set up a mini obstacle course in your backyard or living room. Use treats as rewards for successfully navigating the course. This not only stimulates their mind but also helps with agility training.

Playful Training Techniques

1. Clicker Training: Clicker training can be both fun and effective. The clicker sound becomes associated with rewards, making your Shiba Inu eager to perform commands to hear that satisfying click.

2. Role Reversal: Let your Shiba Inu take the lead sometimes. Allow them to initiate play and choose which commands to work on. This empowers them and adds an element of unpredictability to training.

3. Dance and Tricks: Teach your Shiba Inu fun tricks like "spin," "shake hands," or even a little dance. These tricks not only provide mental stimulation but are also great for bonding.

Training your Shiba Inu doesn't have to be a dull or rigid process. By infusing play, treats, and a sense of adventure into your training sessions, you'll find that both you and your Shiba Inu look forward to each session. Remember that patience, positive reinforcement, and lots of praise are key to fostering a happy and well-trained Shiba Inu. Enjoy the journey of training together, and you'll build a strong and lasting bond with your furry friend.

No Punishment in Training

In the world of Shiba Inu training, it's crucial to remember one fundamental principle: no punishment. While it may be tempting to resort to punitive methods when your Shiba Inu isn't behaving as desired, it's important to understand why positive reinforcement techniques are more effective and humane. In this chapter, we will explore why punishment should be avoided and how to achieve great results through positive reinforcement.

Understanding Punishment

Punishment-based training methods involve the use of aversive techniques such as yelling, physical corrections, or shock collars to discourage unwanted behavior. While these methods may appear effective in the short term, they often lead to long-term problems such as fear, anxiety, and aggression in your Shiba Inu. Here's why punishment is counterproductive:

1. Fear and Anxiety: Punishing your Shiba Inu can create fear and anxiety, damaging the trust and bond between you and your dog. This can lead to a stressed and unhappy pet.

2. Avoidance Behavior: Instead of learning what's expected, dogs subjected to punishment often learn to avoid the person administering the punishment. This doesn't promote a positive learning experience.

3. Unintended Consequences: Punishment can result in unforeseen consequences. For example, if you punish your

Shiba Inu for growling, they may stop growling but still feel threatened, which could escalate into a bite without warning.

The Power of Positive Reinforcement

Positive reinforcement focuses on rewarding desired behaviors instead of punishing unwanted ones. It involves using treats, praise, toys, and other positive stimuli to encourage your Shiba Inu to behave in a particular way. Here's why positive reinforcement is effective:

1. Builds Trust: Positive reinforcement fosters trust and strengthens the bond between you and your Shiba Inu. They learn to associate you with positive experiences.

2. Clear Communication: It provides clear communication about what behaviors you expect. Your Shiba Inu will willingly perform the desired actions to earn rewards.

3. Boosts Confidence: Positive reinforcement boosts your Shiba Inu's confidence and encourages them to engage in training willingly. They become eager learners rather than fearful or reluctant participants.

Practical Positive Reinforcement

1. Use Treats: Reward your Shiba Inu with small, tasty treats when they obey commands or exhibit good behavior. Treats are immediate and effective reinforcers.

2. Verbal Praise: Offer verbal praise in an upbeat and enthusiastic tone. Your Shiba Inu will appreciate your approval and associate it with their actions.

3. Play and Toys: Incorporate playtime and toys as rewards for a job well done. Interactive play reinforces the bond between you and your dog.

4. Consistency: Be consistent with your rewards and timing. Always reward the behavior you want, even if it's small progress.

In the world of Shiba Inu training, the path to success is paved with positivity and patience. By avoiding punishment and embracing positive reinforcement techniques, you'll not only have a happier and more confident Shiba Inu but also enjoy a stronger and more trusting relationship with your furry friend. Remember, the journey of training should be a joyful one for both you and your Shiba Inu, filled with love and understanding.

Body Language & Voice

Effective Shiba Inu training goes beyond just the commands and treats; it involves understanding and mastering the art of communication through body language and voice. Your Shiba Inu is highly attuned to your cues, and in this chapter, we'll explore how to harness the power of your body language and voice to create a successful and harmonious training experience.

The Importance of Non-Verbal Communication

Dogs, including Shiba Inus, rely heavily on non-verbal cues to understand the world around them. Here are some key reasons why mastering body language and voice is essential in training:

1. Clear Communication: Your body language and tone of voice can help convey your expectations and reinforce your commands. Clear signals make it easier for your Shiba Inu to understand what you want.

2. Bond and Trust: Positive body language and a calm voice build trust and strengthen the bond between you and your dog. When they feel safe and comfortable, they are more likely to cooperate.

3. Emotion Regulation: Your Shiba Inu is adept at reading your emotional state. By controlling your body language and voice, you can help your dog remain calm and focused, even in challenging situations.

Body Language Tips

1. Maintain Eye Contact:

Establish and maintain eye contact with your Shiba Inu during training. It conveys attentiveness and helps them stay engaged.

2. Posture and Stance:

Stand upright with a relaxed but confident posture. Avoid looming over your dog, as it may be perceived as threatening.

3. Use Hand Signals:

Combine hand signals with verbal commands to reinforce your message. For example, use an open hand and upward motion for "sit."

4. Gesture with Purpose: Be intentional with your gestures. Avoid confusing or erratic movements that may distract your Shiba Inu.

5. Stay Calm: Keep your movements calm and deliberate, especially when your Shiba Inu is learning something new. Patience is key.

Voice Control Tips

1. Tone of Voice: Use a consistent and calm tone of voice. High-pitched voices can convey excitement, while a lower, firm tone is more appropriate for correction.

2. Clear Commands: Pronounce commands clearly and consistently. Use the same words each time to avoid confusion.

3. Timing: Time your commands and praise appropriately. Give commands before your Shiba Inu performs an action, and praise immediately when they follow through.

4. Avoid Yelling: Yelling or shouting at your Shiba Inu can create fear and confusion. Instead, use a firm tone when necessary.

Building Trust and Confidence

Training is not just about teaching your Shiba Inu commands; it's about creating a positive and trusting relationship. Here are some final tips to keep in mind:

1. Positive Reinforcement: Always pair your body language and voice with positive reinforcement techniques we discussed in previous chapters.

2. Consistency: Be consistent in your signals and voice commands. This helps your Shiba Inu understand what is expected of them.

3. Practice Patience: Training takes time, and every dog learns at their own pace. Be patient and understanding throughout the process.

4. Observe Your Shiba Inu: Pay attention to your dog's body language as well. Their reactions can give you valuable insights into their feelings and understanding.

Mastering the art of body language and voice in Shiba Inu training is an essential skill that will lead to effective communication, trust, and a harmonious relationship with your furry companion. By using clear and consistent cues and maintaining a calm and positive demeanor, you'll set the stage for successful and enjoyable training sessions. Remember, your Shiba Inu is eager to understand and please you, so make every effort to be a clear and empathetic teacher.

Rewards and Treats

Rewards and treats are powerful tools when it comes to training your Shiba Inu. In this chapter, we'll explore how to effectively use rewards, including treats, to motivate and reinforce desired behaviors. With the right approach, you can make training a delightful and rewarding experience for both you and your Shiba Inu.

The Role of Rewards

Rewards play a pivotal role in Shiba Inu training for several reasons:

1. Motivation: Rewards serve as motivation for your Shiba Inu to perform the desired behavior. They provide an incentive to engage in training actively.

2. Positive Reinforcement: Rewards are a key component of positive reinforcement, which is a gentle and effective training method. Positive reinforcement encourages your Shiba Inu to repeat behaviors that earn them rewards.

3. Communication: Rewards help communicate to your Shiba Inu that they've done something right. This clear feedback accelerates the learning process.

4. Bonding: Offering rewards is a way to strengthen your bond with your Shiba Inu. It builds trust and a sense of cooperation.

Choosing the Right Treats

When selecting treats for training, keep the following guidelines in mind:

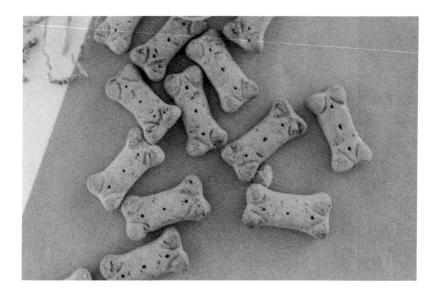

1. Size Matters: Opt for small treats that your Shiba Inu can quickly eat and won't fill them up. You want treats that are bite-sized and easy to manage during training sessions.

2. High Value vs. Low Value: Reserve high-value treats (the most delicious ones) for more challenging commands or new behaviors. Use lower-value treats for reinforcing known commands.

3. Variety: Mix up the types of treats you use to keep your Shiba Inu engaged and excited. Try soft treats, crunchy treats, and even pieces of their regular kibble.

4. Healthy Choices: Ensure that the treats you choose are healthy and appropriate for your Shiba Inu's dietary needs.

Avoid treats with excessive fillers, additives, or preservatives.

Timing Is Crucial

Timing is everything when it comes to rewarding your Shiba Inu during training:

1. Immediate Reward: Give the reward immediately after your Shiba Inu performs the desired behavior. This reinforces the connection between the action and the reward.

2. Consistency: Be consistent in your timing. The reward should be given at the exact moment your Shiba Inu complies with the command.

3. Use a Marker: Consider using a marker word (like "yes" or "good") to signal that the reward is coming. This helps your Shiba Inu understand which behavior is being rewarded.

Gradual Phasing

As your Shiba Inu becomes more proficient in following commands, you can gradually reduce the frequency of treats:

1. Intermittent Reinforcement: Instead of treating every time, use intermittent reinforcement. Randomly reward your Shiba Inu for good behavior to maintain their motivation.

2. Transition to Praise: Over time, replace some treats with verbal praise or petting. Your Shiba Inu will still feel rewarded by your positive attention.

3. Keep It Fun: Always make training enjoyable for your Shiba Inu. The goal is for them to associate training with fun and positive experiences.

Benefiting from Proper Education

In the world of Shiba Inu training, knowledge is power. Understanding the principles of dog behavior and training techniques is the cornerstone of a successful partnership with your furry friend. In this chapter, we'll explore the advantages of educating yourself about proper training methods, and how this knowledge can transform your training sessions with your Shiba Inu.

The Value of Education

Before delving into the specific benefits of proper education in dog training, let's emphasize why it matters:

1. Effective Communication: Learning about canine behavior and training methods enables you to communicate effectively with your Shiba Inu. You'll understand their needs, tendencies, and how to convey your expectations clearly.

2. Builds Confidence: When you're well-informed, you'll feel more confident as a trainer. Confidence is contagious and can positively impact your Shiba Inu's trust in your leadership.

3. Problem Solving: Education equips you with problem-solving skills. You'll be better prepared to address challenges that arise during training, ensuring a smoother process.

4. Enhances Bond: Knowledge-based training enhances the bond between you and your Shiba Inu. Your dog will recognize your competence and trust your guidance.

Understanding Canine Behavior

To benefit from proper education in Shiba Inu training, start by understanding canine behavior:

1. Learn about Breed Characteristics: Study the unique traits and characteristics of Shiba Inus. Understanding their breed-specific behaviors will help you tailor your training approach.

2. Body Language: Familiarize yourself with canine body language. Recognizing signs of stress, anxiety, or contentment will help you gauge your Shiba Inu's emotional state during training.

3. Socialization: Understand the importance of socialization. Proper socialization during puppyhood can prevent behavioral issues later on.

4. Positive Reinforcement: Educate yourself on positive reinforcement training techniques. This approach is proven to be effective, humane, and builds trust with your Shiba Inu.

Practical Benefits of Education

1. Training Efficiency: Proper education allows you to train your Shiba Inu more efficiently. You'll know how to structure sessions, set achievable goals, and track progress.

2. Problem Prevention: Knowledge of canine behavior enables you to anticipate and prevent behavioral issues before they escalate. You'll spot signs of trouble early and take corrective action.

3. Adaptability: As you learn more about training methods and principles, you can adapt your approach to your Shiba Inu's individual needs and personality.

4. Confidence in Corrections: If corrections are ever necessary, education ensures that you apply them correctly and fairly. You'll understand when and how to correct behaviors without resorting to punishment.

Resources for Education

1. Books: There are numerous books on dog behavior and training written by experts in the field. Look for well-reviewed titles that align with your training philosophy.

2. Online Courses: Many reputable dog trainers offer online courses and resources that can help you expand your knowledge and skills.

3. Local Classes: Consider enrolling in local dog training classes. These provide hands-on experience and guidance from experienced trainers.

4. Professional Trainers: Consult with professional dog trainers for personalized guidance and advice.

Preparation & Planning

Successful Shiba Inu training doesn't happen by chance; it's the result of careful preparation and thoughtful planning. In this chapter, we'll delve into the importance of getting ready for training sessions and how a well-thought-out approach can make a significant difference in achieving your training goals.

The Foundation of Effective Training

Before you even start a training session with your Shiba Inu, it's essential to lay a solid foundation. Here's why preparation and planning are crucial:

1. Clarity: Preparation helps you define clear training goals and objectives. Knowing what you want to achieve is the first step towards success.

2. Efficiency: A well-prepared session is more efficient. You'll use your time effectively, making the most of both yours and your Shiba Inu's efforts.

3. Consistency: Planning ensures consistency in your training approach. A consistent routine helps your Shiba Inu understand what's expected of them.

4. Adaptability: A prepared trainer is better equipped to adapt to unexpected challenges during training. You'll be able to modify your plan as needed without getting frustrated.

Steps for Preparation and Planning

Let's explore the essential steps to prepare for successful Shiba Inu training sessions:

1. Define Your Goals: Before each training session, clearly define your goals. Ask yourself what specific behavior or command you want to work on. Setting achievable goals keeps your training focused and productive.

2. Gather Training Tools: Ensure you have all the necessary tools and resources on hand. This may include treats, a leash, a clicker, toys, and any props required for specific training exercises.

3. Choose the Right Environment: Select a suitable training environment. It should be quiet, free from distractions, and safe for your Shiba Inu. A familiar place where your dog feels comfortable is ideal.

4. Plan Session Duration: Decide on the duration of your training session. Keep it short and focused, especially for younger Shiba Inus. Aim for 10-15 minute sessions to maintain your dog's interest and attention.

5. Prepare Your Dog: Before starting training, make sure your Shiba Inu is in the right state of mind. They should be calm and not overly excited or tired. A short walk or playtime to release excess energy can be helpful.

6. Create a Training Plan: Outline a training plan for the session. Break down the behavior or command into smaller, manageable steps. Start with the basics and gradually progress to more complex tasks.

7. Be Consistent: Consistency is key to successful training. Ensure that everyone in your household is on the same page regarding training methods and commands. Consistency reinforces learning.

8. Prepare for Rewards: Have your rewards, such as treats or toys, readily accessible. You don't want to waste time fumbling for rewards during the session.

9. Stay Positive: Maintain a positive and upbeat attitude throughout the training session. Your enthusiasm and encouragement will motivate your Shiba Inu.

10. Evaluate and Adjust: After each session, take a moment to evaluate your progress. Did you achieve your goals? What worked well, and what needs improvement? Adjust your plan accordingly for future sessions.

Socialization

Socialization is a critical aspect of raising a well-rounded and well-behaved Shiba Inu. In this chapter, we'll explore the importance of socialization, starting with general socialization, moving on to puppy socialization, and then addressing the unique challenges of socializing your Shiba Inu with other animals.

General Socialization

Socialization is the process of exposing your Shiba Inu to a wide variety of people, places, sights, sounds, and experiences in a positive and controlled manner. This early exposure helps your dog develop confidence and adaptability. Here's why general socialization matters:

1. Behavioral Development: Early socialization lays the foundation for your Shiba Inu's behavior. It helps prevent fearfulness, aggression, and anxiety in various situations.

2. Positive Associations: Exposure to new things in a positive context helps your Shiba Inu form positive associations with novel experiences.

3. Life Skills: Socialization teaches your dog life skills such as how to interact with strangers, other dogs, and adapt to different environments.

4. Improved Training: Well-socialized dogs are often more receptive to training because they are less anxious and more focused.

To properly socialize your Shiba Inu, introduce them to different environments, people, and experiences gradually, always using positive reinforcement and rewards.

Puppy Socialization

Puppy socialization is a critical phase in your Shiba Inu's development. It typically occurs between the ages of 3 weeks and 14-16 weeks. During this time, your Shiba Inu is more receptive to new experiences, making it an ideal period for socialization. Here's how to approach it:

1. Safe Exposure: Introduce your puppy to various people, including children and strangers. Ensure these interactions are safe and positive.

2. Different Environments: Take your puppy to different environments like parks, pet-friendly stores, and quiet streets. Gradually increase the level of stimulation.

3. Other Dogs: Arrange controlled playdates with other puppies or well-behaved adult dogs. Early positive experiences with other dogs are crucial.

4. Handling: Get your puppy accustomed to being handled by gently touching their paws, ears, and tail. This helps with grooming and vet visits.

5. Training Classes: Enroll your Shiba Inu in puppy training classes. These classes provide structured socialization opportunities and teach basic obedience.

Socialization with Other Animals

Shiba Inus can be independent and have strong prey instincts, making socializing them with other animals a unique challenge. Here's how to approach this type of socialization:

1. Gradual Introduction: When introducing your Shiba Inu to other animals, do so gradually and under supervision. Start with calm, well-behaved animals.

2. Positive Reinforcement: Reward your Shiba Inu for calm and appropriate behavior around other animals. Use treats and praise to reinforce good conduct.

3. Obedience Training: Ensure your Shiba Inu has solid obedience training, including commands like "leave it" and "stay." These commands are invaluable when socializing with other animals.

4. Professional Guidance: If you're unsure about how to socialize your Shiba Inu with other animals, seek guidance from a professional dog trainer experienced in this area.

5. Monitor Interactions: Always supervise interactions between your Shiba Inu and other animals, especially in the early stages of socialization.

Socialization is an ongoing process that significantly contributes to your Shiba Inu's well-being and behavior. Starting with general socialization, followed by focused puppy socialization, and addressing the unique challenges of socializing with other animals, you'll help your Shiba Inu become a well-adjusted and confident companion.

Problems

Problems

Chapter Two

Dealing with Fear & Other Behavior Issues

While Shiba Inus are generally known for their spirited personalities, they may occasionally exhibit behavior issues such as aggression, fearfulness, or anxiety. In this chapter, we'll explore how to recognize and address these problems effectively, ensuring a harmonious relationship with your Shiba Inu.

Understanding Behavior Issues

It's important to remember that behavior issues in Shiba Inus, like any breed, can arise for various reasons, including genetics, past experiences, or lack of proper socialization. Common behavior issues include aggression, fearfulness, separation anxiety, and more.

Recognizing Aggression

Aggressive behavior in Shiba Inus can manifest in various ways, including growling, snapping, or biting. It's crucial to identify the triggers and understand the type of aggression your Shiba Inu may display:

Fear Aggression: This occurs when your Shiba Inu perceives a threat and responds aggressively as a defense mechanism.

Territorial Aggression: Shiba Inus can be protective of their territory and may become aggressive toward intruders or other animals.

Resource Guarding: Aggression may arise when your dog guards valuable resources like food, toys, or even your attention.

Dog-Dog Aggression: Some Shiba Inus may be aggressive towards other dogs, particularly of the same sex.

Dealing with Aggression

Addressing aggression in your Shiba Inu requires a careful and patient approach:

Consult a Professional: If your Shiba Inu displays aggressive behavior, it's essential to seek guidance from a professional dog trainer or behaviorist with experience in aggression cases.

Safety First: Prioritize safety for yourself, your dog, and others. Avoid situations that trigger aggression until you can address the issue with professional help.

Positive Reinforcement: Use positive reinforcement techniques to encourage calm and non-aggressive behavior. Reward your Shiba Inu for remaining composed in challenging situations.

Counterconditioning: Counterconditioning involves changing your dog's emotional response to a trigger. For example, rewarding your Shiba Inu when they see another dog without reacting aggressively can gradually reduce their fear or aggression.

Addressing Fear and Anxiety

Fear and anxiety are common problems in Shiba Inus, leading to behaviors like excessive barking, trembling, or withdrawal. Here's how to approach these issues:

Identify Triggers: Determine the specific situations or stimuli that trigger fear or anxiety in your Shiba Inu.

Desensitization: Gradually expose your Shiba Inu to the trigger in a controlled and positive manner to reduce their fear.

Counterconditioning: Pair the trigger with something positive, like treats or play, to change your dog's emotional response.

Create a Safe Space: Provide a safe and comfortable space where your Shiba Inu can retreat when feeling anxious.

Professional Help: For severe cases of fear and anxiety, consider consulting a professional dog behaviorist who can develop a tailored behavior modification plan.

Addressing aggression, fear, or other behavior issues in your Shiba Inu requires patience, understanding, and often professional guidance. By recognizing the signs and triggers, using positive reinforcement techniques, and seeking expert help when necessary, you can work towards resolving these challenges and ensure a happy and well-adjusted Shiba Inu. Remember, addressing behavior issues is an ongoing process, and with dedication, you can improve your dog's quality of life and strengthen your bond.

Addressing Nipping, Jumping & Running Off

Shiba Inus, like many dogs, may exhibit a range of challenging behaviors that can test your patience. In this chapter, we'll tackle common issues such as nipping, chewing, jumping, pulling, disobedience, whining, howling, and running off, providing you with strategies to manage and correct these behaviors effectively.

Nipping

Nipping is a common behavior issue in Shiba Inu puppies, especially during play. Here's how to address it:

Teach Bite Inhibition: Encourage gentle mouthing by yelping when your puppy nips too hard. Gradually, they'll learn to control their bite.

Redirect with Toys: Have plenty of chew toys on hand to redirect your puppy's biting instincts. Praise and reward them for chewing on toys instead of your hands.

Consistent Training: Be consistent in discouraging nipping. Always reinforce the "gentle" command and praise when your Shiba Inu follows it.

Chewing

Shiba Inus, particularly puppies, love to chew to soothe teething discomfort or out of boredom. To manage chewing behavior:

Provide Appropriate Chew Toys: Offer a variety of durable and safe chew toys. Rotate them to keep your Shiba Inu engaged.

Supervise and Confine: Supervise your dog when they are loose in the house and use baby gates to restrict access to off-limits areas.

Puppy-Proof Your Home: Remove valuable or hazardous items from your Shiba Inu's reach to prevent destruction.

Jumping

Shiba Inus are active dogs that may exhibit jumping behavior, especially when excited. To address jumping:

Ignore and Reward Calm Behavior: Turn away and avoid eye contact when your dog jumps on you. Reward and praise them once they are calm with all four paws on the ground.

Teach "Off" or "Down" Command: Train your Shiba Inu to respond to the "off" or "down" command, and reward them for complying.

Consistency: Enforce consistent rules with family members and visitors to prevent mixed signals.

Pulling on the Leash

Shiba Inus can be strong-willed and may pull on the leash during walks. To discourage this behavior:

Use Proper Equipment: Consider a no-pull harness or head collar to provide better control during walks.

Training: Practice loose-leash walking by stopping and changing direction whenever your Shiba Inu pulls. Reward them when they walk without tension on the leash.

Consistency: Be patient and consistent in your training efforts. Practice regularly to reinforce good leash manners.

Disobedience

Shiba Inus can be independent, leading to occasional disobedience. To address disobedience:

Positive Reinforcement: Use positive reinforcement to motivate your Shiba Inu to obey commands. Reward desired behaviors generously.

Obedience Training: Invest time in obedience training, focusing on basic commands like "sit," "stay," and "come." Consistency is key.

Stay Calm: Maintain a calm and assertive demeanor when issuing commands. Avoid frustration or anger.

Whining, Howling, and Running Off

Whining, howling, and running off can be challenging behaviors to address. Here's how to handle them:

Understand the Cause: Determine the underlying cause of whining, howling, or running off. It may be due to boredom, anxiety, or a need for exercise.

Exercise and Mental Stimulation: Ensure your Shiba Inu receives enough physical exercise and mental stimulation to prevent restlessness.

Desensitization: For separation anxiety, desensitize your Shiba Inu to your departures by leaving for short periods and gradually increasing the time.

Professional Help: Seek professional assistance if these behaviors persist, as they may require specialized training.

Addressing these challenging behaviors in your Shiba Inu requires patience, consistency, and positive reinforcement. By understanding the underlying causes and using appropriate training techniques, you can effectively manage and correct these issues, fostering a well-behaved and happy canine companion. Remember that every dog is unique, so tailor your approach to your Shiba Inu's specific needs and personality.

Housetraining & Barking Behavior

Housetraining and managing barking behavior are essential aspects of raising a well-behaved Shiba Inu. In this chapter, we'll explore strategies to ensure your Shiba Inu becomes housetrained and understands appropriate barking behavior.

Housetraining

Housetraining, also known as potty training, is one of the first skills you should teach your Shiba Inu. Consistency and patience are key to success:

Establish a Routine

Regular Schedule: Take your Shiba Inu outside at regular intervals, especially after waking up, eating, drinking, and playtime.

Praise and Reward: When your Shiba Inu eliminates outside, praise and reward them immediately. Use treats or verbal praise to reinforce the desired behavior.

Supervise and Anticipate: Keep a close eye on your dog indoors, especially when they are not yet housetrained. Watch for signs like sniffing, circling, or whining, which may indicate they need to go out.

Crate Training: Use a crate to prevent accidents when you can't supervise your Shiba Inu. Dogs are less likely to eliminate where they sleep, so the crate can be an effective housetraining tool.

Accidents Happen: Be prepared for accidents; they are a normal part of the housetraining process. Clean up accidents promptly with an enzymatic cleaner to remove odors.

Avoid Punishment

Never scold or punish your Shiba Inu for accidents indoors. This can create fear and anxiety, hindering the housetraining process.

Patience and Persistence

Housetraining takes time, and every dog progresses at their own pace. Be patient and persistent, and your Shiba Inu will eventually become reliably housetrained.

Barking Behavior

Shiba Inus are known for their vocal nature, but excessive or inappropriate barking can be a nuisance. Here's how to manage barking behavior:

Identify the Cause

Understand the Triggers: Pay attention to what causes your Shiba Inu to bark. Is it boredom, excitement, fear, or territorial behavior?

Separation Anxiety: If your Shiba Inu barks excessively when left alone, they may be experiencing separation anxiety. Consult a professional if this is the case.

Training and Management

Basic Obedience: Teach your Shiba Inu basic obedience commands like "quiet" or "enough." Reward them when they stop barking on command.

Positive Distraction: Provide toys or puzzles that can keep your dog mentally engaged and reduce boredom-related barking.

Exercise: Ensure your Shiba Inu gets enough physical exercise and mental stimulation. A tired dog is less likely to bark excessively.

Socialization: Socialize your Shiba Inu from an early age to help reduce fear-related barking.

Consistency

Consistency is crucial when addressing barking behavior. Enforce consistent rules within your household, so your Shiba Inu knows what is expected of them.

Seek Professional Help

If your Shiba Inu's barking behavior is causing significant problems or is difficult to manage, consider consulting a professional dog trainer or behaviorist for personalized guidance.

Housetraining and managing barking behavior are essential components of responsible Shiba Inu ownership. By establishing a consistent routine, using positive reinforcement, and understanding the reasons behind your Shiba Inu's behavior, you can successfully housetrain your dog and promote appropriate barking behavior. Remember that patience, understanding, and training are key to achieving these goals and ensuring a happy and well-adjusted Shiba Inu.

Effective Discipline

Effective discipline is a vital component of Shiba Inu training, helping to establish boundaries and reinforce desirable behaviors. In this chapter, we'll explore the principles of effective discipline that maintain your Shiba Inu's respect while fostering a positive and cooperative relationship.

Understanding Discipline

Discipline should never be about punishment or causing fear. Instead, it's about teaching your Shiba Inu what is acceptable behavior and what is not. Here are the key principles of effective discipline:

Consistency: Consistency is paramount in discipline. Set clear rules and expectations, and ensure everyone in your household follows them consistently. Inconsistency can lead to confusion and undesirable behaviors.

Timing: Timing is crucial when correcting behavior. Address issues immediately or as soon as possible to connect the correction with the behavior. Delayed discipline may confuse your Shiba Inu.

Positive Reinforcement: While discipline involves correcting unwanted behaviors, it should be balanced with positive reinforcement. Praise and reward your Shiba Inu for displaying desired behaviors. Positive reinforcement helps your dog understand what behaviors are rewarded and encourages them to repeat those actions.

Fairness: Discipline should always be fair and proportional to the behavior. Avoid harsh punishments or overreacting to minor infractions. The discipline should match the severity of the action.

Redirect: Instead of simply scolding your Shiba Inu, redirect their behavior to something more appropriate. For example, if your Shiba Inu is chewing on furniture, give them a chew toy as an alternative.

Techniques for Effective Discipline

Here are some effective discipline techniques to use when necessary:

Verbal Commands: Use clear and consistent verbal commands to correct behavior. For example, if your Shiba Inu is jumping on people, say "off" firmly and then praise and reward when they comply.

Time-Outs: A time-out involves briefly isolating your Shiba Inu as a consequence for undesirable behavior. Place them in a quiet, non-stimulating area for a short time, then allow them to rejoin the family when they've calmed down.

Withdraw Attention: Withdrawing attention is a powerful way to discipline unwanted behaviors like barking or whining. When your Shiba Inu engages in the undesirable behavior, simply turn away and ignore them. Reward and praise when they stop.

Ignore: For attention-seeking behaviors, ignoring can be effective. If your Shiba Inu begs for attention by barking or pawing, refrain from giving them attention until they are calm and quiet.

Use a Stern Tone: A stern tone of voice can convey your disapproval without resorting to harsh punishment. Your Shiba Inu can pick up on your tone and understand that they need to correct their behavior.

The Importance of Positive Reinforcement

While discipline is essential, it should be used in conjunction with positive reinforcement. Positive reinforcement strengthens desired behaviors and builds a trusting and cooperative relationship with your Shiba Inu.

Remember that discipline is about guiding and teaching your Shiba Inu, not about causing fear or harm. Effective discipline techniques help create a well-behaved and happy Shiba Inu while maintaining a loving and respectful bond between you and your furry friend.

How Long is Too Long to Leave Alone?

As a responsible Shiba Inu owner, it's crucial to consider your dog's well-being when determining how long you can leave them alone. In this chapter, we'll explore the factors that influence how long is too long to leave your Shiba Inu at home and offer guidelines for ensuring their happiness and health.

Shiba Inus and Alone Time

Shiba Inus are known for their independent nature, but they still require social interaction and mental stimulation. Leaving them alone for extended periods can lead to several issues, including:

Boredom: Boredom can result in destructive behavior, excessive barking, and anxiety.

Separation Anxiety: Shiba Inus are prone to separation anxiety when left alone for too long, leading to stress and emotional distress.

Housebreaking Regression: Prolonged periods of confinement can hinder housebreaking progress.

Loneliness: Dogs are social animals and thrive on human and canine companionship.

Factors to Consider

The appropriate duration your Shiba Inu can be left alone depends on several factors:

Age

Puppy: Puppies require more attention and cannot be left alone for long. They need frequent bathroom breaks, playtime, and socialization.

Adult: Adult Shiba Inus can generally handle longer periods alone, but they still need daily exercise and mental stimulation.

Health

Consider your Shiba Inu's health. Dogs with medical conditions may require more frequent care and monitoring.

Exercise

Shiba Inus are an active breed and need daily exercise. If they don't get enough physical activity, they may become restless and engage in undesirable behaviors.

Mental Stimulation

Mental stimulation is essential for preventing boredom. Provide puzzle toys, interactive games, and training sessions to keep your Shiba Inu mentally engaged.

Training

Well-trained dogs tend to handle alone time better. Teaching your Shiba Inu basic obedience and commands like "stay" and "quiet" can be helpful.

Socialization

Shiba Inus benefit from socialization with other dogs. Consider arranging playdates or doggy daycare to provide social interaction when you're away.

Guidelines for Leaving Your Shiba Inu Alone

While every Shiba Inu is unique, here are some general guidelines for how long you can leave your Shiba Inu alone:

Puppies (8-16 Weeks Old): Puppies of this age cannot be left alone for more than 1-2 hours at a time. They require frequent bathroom breaks, play, and supervision.

Puppies (4-6 Months Old): At this age, you can leave your puppy alone for 2-4 hours. Ensure they have a safe and confined space.

Adults (6 Months and Older): Adult Shiba Inus can typically handle 4-8 hours alone, depending on their individual needs. Provide exercise and mental stimulation before and after your absence.

Alternatives to Extended Alone Time

If your schedule requires you to be away for longer periods, consider these alternatives:

Dog Sitter: Hire a dog sitter or enlist a trusted friend or family member to check on your Shiba Inu during the day.

Doggy Daycare: Enroll your Shiba Inu in a reputable doggy daycare for socialization and supervision.

Professional Dog Walker: Hire a professional dog walker to provide exercise and companionship during your absence.

Interactive Toys: Provide interactive toys and puzzle feeders to keep your Shiba Inu mentally engaged while you're away.

Pet Cameras: Use pet cameras to check on your dog and even interact with them remotely.

It's important to strike a balance between your daily responsibilities and your Shiba Inu's needs. While they can tolerate some alone time, consider their age, health, and activity level when determining how long is too long to leave them alone. Always prioritize their well-being, and you'll ensure a happy and well-adjusted companion.

Common Mistakes Made by Owners

In our journey to train and care for our Shiba Inus, it's important to be aware of common mistakes that owners can make. In this chapter, we'll explore some of these mistakes and offer guidance on how to avoid them to ensure a happy and well-adjusted Shiba Inu.

Inadequate Socialization

One of the most common mistakes is not providing enough socialization for your Shiba Inu, especially during the critical puppy phase. Failure to expose your dog to various people, animals, and environments can lead to fearfulness and behavioral issues later in life.

Avoidance: Make socialization a priority from an early age. Gradually introduce your Shiba Inu to different situations, people, and animals to build their confidence and adaptability.

Inconsistent Training

Inconsistency in training can lead to confusion for your Shiba Inu. Using different commands or allowing behaviors at times and not others can hinder progress.

Correction: Establish consistent rules and commands within your household. Ensure that everyone interacting with your Shiba Inu follows the same training guidelines to avoid mixed signals.

Lack of Exercise and Mental Stimulation

Shiba Inus are an active breed, and not providing enough physical exercise and mental stimulation can result in boredom and unwanted behaviors.

Solution: Prioritize daily exercise and engage your Shiba Inu's mind with interactive toys, puzzles, and training sessions. A tired dog is a well-behaved dog.

Overindulging or Overprotecting

Spoiling your Shiba Inu with too many treats or allowing them to get away with inappropriate behaviors can lead to entitlement and disobedience.

Correction: Use treats and rewards selectively, and avoid overindulging your Shiba Inu. Enforce consistent rules and boundaries to maintain a respectful relationship.

Punishment-Based Training

Using punishment-based training methods can lead to fear and aggression in Shiba Inus, eroding trust and causing behavioral issues.

Alternative Approach: Embrace positive reinforcement training, which rewards good behavior rather than punishing bad behavior. This approach builds trust and cooperation with your Shiba Inu.

Neglecting Health and Grooming

Neglecting your Shiba Inu's health and grooming needs can result in discomfort and health issues.

Solution: Regularly check your dog's coat, nails, and ears. Schedule routine vet visits and maintain a healthy diet and exercise regimen for your Shiba Inu.

Inadequate Housetraining

Failing to establish a consistent housetraining routine can lead to accidents and setbacks in the housetraining process.

Prevention: Set a strict housetraining schedule, supervise your Shiba Inu closely, and provide positive reinforcement when they eliminate outdoors. Be patient, as housetraining takes time.

Not Recognizing Individual Needs

Every Shiba Inu is unique, and failing to recognize and adapt to their individual needs can lead to frustration and behavioral problems.

Solution: Pay attention to your Shiba Inu's personality, energy level, and preferences. Adjust your training and care routines accordingly to ensure their happiness and well-being.

Awareness of common mistakes made by Shiba Inu owners is the first step toward being a responsible and effective caregiver. By avoiding these pitfalls and embracing positive, consistent, and attentive training and care, you can create a loving, trusting, and harmonious relationship with your Shiba Inu. Remember that patience, understanding, and a commitment to your dog's needs are the keys to success in raising a happy and well-adjusted companion.

Adult vs. Puppy Shiba Inus

The decision to bring a Shiba Inu into your life comes with various considerations, one of the most significant being whether to adopt an adult dog or a puppy. In this chapter, we'll explore the differences between adult and puppy Shiba Inus, helping you make an informed choice that aligns with your lifestyle and preferences.

Adult Shiba Inus

Personality and Temperament

Steady Temperament: Adult Shiba Inus typically have a more stable temperament compared to puppies. Their personalities are already developed, making it easier to predict their behavior.

Training History: Many adult Shiba Inus may already have basic obedience training or socialization experience, which can simplify the training process.

Known Behavior: You can have a better understanding of their behavior and any specific issues they may have, as these are often known from their previous homes.

Exercise and Activity

Energy Level: While Shiba Inus are naturally active, adult dogs may have slightly lower energy levels compared to puppies, making them more adaptable to your daily routine.

Exercise Requirements: Adult Shiba Inus still need daily exercise but may not require as much playtime as puppies.

Independence

More Independent: Adult Shiba Inus tend to be more independent and may be less demanding of constant attention compared to puppies.

Alone Time: They can generally handle longer periods of alone time without becoming anxious or restless.

Puppy Shiba Inus

Training Potential

Blank Slate: Puppies offer a blank slate for training, allowing you to shape their behaviors and habits from scratch.

Socialization: Early socialization is crucial for puppies, and it's an opportunity to expose them to various experiences and people.

Energy and Playfulness: Puppies are known for their boundless energy and playfulness, which can be infectious and entertaining.

Challenges

Time and Effort: Raising a puppy requires a significant time commitment, including housebreaking, basic training, and socialization efforts.

Patience: Puppies can be challenging and may test your patience with behaviors like nipping, chewing, and house accidents.

Unpredictability: Their adult personality and behavior may not fully develop until around 1-2 years of age, making it difficult to predict their long-term temperament.

Making the Choice

The decision between adopting an adult or a puppy Shiba Inu ultimately depends on your lifestyle, preferences, and circumstances. Here are some considerations to help you choose:

Time and Commitment: Do you have the time and commitment required to raise and train a puppy? Puppies demand more attention and effort in their formative months.

Training Goals: Consider your training goals. If you prefer a dog with a known temperament and some training foundation, an adult Shiba Inu may be a better fit.

Energy Level: Think about your activity level and whether you can match the energy and exercise needs of a puppy or if you prefer a dog with a more moderate energy level.

Previous Experience: Your previous experience with dogs can also influence your decision. First-time dog owners may find it easier to start with an adult dog.

Family Dynamics: Consider your family dynamics and the preferences of everyone in your household. Some family members may have specific preferences for a puppy or an adult dog.

Both adult and puppy Shiba Inus can make wonderful companions, each with its unique advantages and challenges. Carefully evaluate your lifestyle, preferences, and capacity to meet the needs of your future furry family member. Whether you choose an adult Shiba Inu with a known history or a playful and impressionable puppy, your commitment and love will undoubtedly create a strong and fulfilling bond with your new companion.

The Activity He Needs & How Much Is Enough

Shiba Inus are known for their energetic and spirited nature. Providing them with the right amount of physical and mental activity is essential for their well-being and happiness. In this chapter, we'll explore the activity requirements of Shiba Inus and how to ensure they get enough exercise and stimulation.

Understanding Shiba Inu Activity Needs

Shiba Inus are an active and agile breed, and their activity needs can vary based on age, health, and individual disposition. Here's what you need to consider:

Age

Puppies: Shiba Inu puppies have boundless energy and require frequent play and exercise to develop their muscles and coordination.

Adults: Adult Shiba Inus need daily exercise to stay healthy and mentally stimulated. They tend to have more manageable energy levels compared to puppies.

Seniors: Senior Shiba Inus may have reduced activity levels due to aging, but they still benefit from gentle exercise to maintain mobility.

Energy Level

High-Energy Dogs: Some Shiba Inus have higher energy levels and may need more vigorous exercise and mental stimulation.

Moderate-Energy Dogs: Others may have a more moderate energy level, requiring a balanced mix of activity and rest.

Exercise Requirements

To meet your Shiba Inu's exercise needs, consider the following activities:

Daily Walks

Frequency: Aim for at least one or two daily walks, depending on your dog's age and energy level.

Duration: Walks should typically last 30 minutes to an hour. Adjust the duration based on your Shiba Inu's fitness level.

Interactive Play

Fetch: Playing fetch is an excellent way to engage your Shiba

Inu's natural hunting instincts and provide both physical and mental exercise.

Tug of War: Tug of war can be a fun and interactive game that helps build your dog's strength and focus.

Hide and Seek: Hide treats or toys around the house for your Shiba Inu to find, stimulating their problem-solving skills.

Off-Leash Time

Dog Parks: If your Shiba Inu is well-socialized and friendly with other dogs, trips to a dog park can be a great way for them to expend energy and socialize.

Secure Areas: Allow your Shiba Inu some off-leash time in secure, fenced areas to explore and run freely.

Mental Stimulation

Puzzle Toys: Provide puzzle toys and treat-dispensing toys to challenge your Shiba Inu's mind.

Training: Regular training sessions not only reinforce obedience but also engage your dog's mental faculties.

Signs of a Well-Exercised Shiba Inu

Calmer Behavior: A well-exercised Shiba Inu is typically calmer and less prone to restlessness or destructive behaviors.

Contentment: Your dog should appear content and satisfied after exercise, often displaying a relaxed posture and demeanor.

Appetite: Exercise can stimulate your Shiba Inu's appetite, which is generally a positive sign.

Overexercising Precautions

While exercise is essential, it's crucial not to overexert your Shiba Inu, especially during extreme weather conditions. Watch for signs of fatigue, overheating, or limping, and adjust their activity accordingly.

Meeting your Shiba Inu's activity needs is essential for their physical and mental well-being. Tailor their exercise regimen to their age, energy level, and individual disposition, ensuring a balance between physical and mental stimulation. By providing your Shiba Inu with the right amount of activity, you'll keep them happy, healthy, and well-adjusted, strengthening the bond between you and your furry companion.

Preparing Training Materials

Effective training for your Shiba Inu begins with proper preparation. In this chapter, we will discuss the essential materials and tools you need to have on hand to make your training sessions productive and successful.

The Importance of Preparation

Before you start any training sessions with your Shiba Inu, it's essential to gather the necessary materials. Being prepared ensures that you can focus on training without interruptions and provides a smooth and organized training experience for both you and your dog.

Training Essentials

Here are the key materials and tools you should have ready for your Shiba Inu's training sessions:

1. Treats or Rewards:

Treats are a fundamental component of positive reinforcement training. Choose small, bite-sized treats that your Shiba Inu finds irresistible. These will serve as rewards for good behavior.

Variety: Have a variety of treats on hand, including high-value treats for more challenging tasks and lower-value treats for routine commands.

Treat Pouch: Consider using a treat pouch or bag that attaches to your waist for easy access during training.

2. Training Leash and Collar or Harness:

A well-fitted leash and collar or harness are crucial for safety and control during training sessions, especially when working on leash-related commands.

Leash: Use a standard leash for basic training exercises and a longer leash for recall or distance training.

Collar or Harness: Ensure your Shiba Inu wears a comfortable and properly fitting collar or harness.

3. Clicker:

A clicker is a handy tool for marking desired behaviors with a distinct sound. While not necessary, many trainers find it helpful for precise communication with their dogs.

Clicker Training: If you choose to use a clicker, familiarize yourself with how it works and practice timing your clicks accurately.

4. Toys and Props

Depending on your training goals, specific toys or props may be helpful.

Interactive Toys: Use toys like balls or tug toys for play-based training exercises.

Agility Equipment: If you're working on agility training, you may need jumps, tunnels, or weave poles.

5. Training Space:

Designate a quiet, distraction-free space for training. Indoor or outdoor areas with minimal noise and interruptions are ideal for focused training sessions.

6. Notepad and Pen:

Keeping a training journal can help track your progress and note any challenges or breakthroughs during your training sessions.

7. Patience and Positive Attitude:

While not physical materials, these are essential for successful training. Maintain a positive attitude and approach each training session with patience and understanding.

Safety Considerations

Always prioritize safety during training. Ensure that your training materials are in good condition, and monitor your Shiba Inu for any signs of discomfort or stress. If you encounter challenges during training, seek professional guidance or consult with a veterinarian to rule out any underlying health issues.

Proper preparation and the right training materials are essential for successful training sessions with your Shiba Inu. Having treats, leashes, toys, and other tools at your disposal will make the training process smoother and more enjoyable for both you and your furry companion. Remember that consistency and positive reinforcement are key elements of effective training, so stay committed and patient throughout your training journey.

Leash & Collar

Chapter Three

Leash and Collar Training

Leash and collar training is a fundamental part of your Shiba Inu's obedience and safety. In this chapter, we will cover the various aspects of leash and collar training, including how they work, teaching your Shiba Inu to accept them, training not to pull, using training leads, and the pros and cons of using collars.

How Leashes and Collars Work

Leash: A leash is a tether that attaches to your Shiba Inu's collar or harness, allowing you to guide and control their movements during walks or training sessions.

Collar: A collar is a wearable device that fits around your Shiba Inu's neck. It can hold identification tags and be used as an attachment point for the leash.

Teaching Your Shiba Inu to Accept the Leash and Collar

Before you start leash and collar training, it's important to ensure your Shiba Inu is comfortable wearing them:

Introduction: Begin by introducing the collar or harness to your Shiba Inu in a calm and positive manner. Allow them to sniff and explore the new item before putting it on.

Positive Associations: Associate the collar or harness with positive experiences by giving treats and praise during and after its placement.

Short Sessions: Initially, keep the collar or harness on for short periods inside the house, gradually increasing the duration as your Shiba Inu becomes more accustomed to it.

Training Not to Pull on the Leash

Leash pulling can be a common issue, but with patience and consistent training, you can teach your Shiba Inu to walk politely on a leash:

Use a Short Leash: Start with a short leash to maintain control.

Practice "Heel": Teach your Shiba Inu the "heel" command, which means walking beside you without pulling.

Positive Reinforcement: Reward your dog with treats and praise when they walk without pulling. Encourage them to stay close by your side.

Stop and Change Direction: If your Shiba Inu starts to pull, stop and change direction. This teaches them that pulling doesn't get them where they want to go.

Be Consistent: Enforce consistent rules during walks. Do not allow your Shiba Inu to pull sometimes and not others.

Training Leads for Dogs

Training leads, also known as long lines or training leashes, can be valuable tools during leash training:

Length: Training leads are typically longer than standard leashes, often ranging from 15 to 50 feet.

Control: They provide greater control over your Shiba Inu while allowing them more freedom to explore during training sessions.

Recall Training: Training leads are particularly useful for recall training, helping your Shiba Inu learn to come when called.

Pros and Cons of Collars

Pros:

Identification: Collars provide a convenient place to attach identification tags with your contact information.

Attachment Point: They serve as a secure attachment point for leashes and other training tools.

Comfort: Well-fitted collars can be comfortable for your Shiba Inu, especially if they have a habit of slipping out of harnesses.

Cons:

Neck Strain: Collars can put pressure on the neck and throat, potentially causing injury or discomfort, especially if your Shiba Inu pulls on the leash.

Limited Control: Collars may offer less control than harnesses, making them less suitable for dogs prone to pulling.

Health Concerns: Some Shiba Inus with certain medical conditions, such as tracheal issues, may be better served by using a harness.

Leash and collar training are essential for the safety and control of your Shiba Inu during walks and training sessions. By patiently introducing your dog to these tools, teaching them not to pull, and using positive reinforcement techniques, you can enjoy pleasant and safe outings with your Shiba Inu. Consider the use of training leads when necessary, and weigh the pros and cons of collars to make the best choice for your dog's needs and comfort.

Training Tools and Aids

Effective training often involves the use of various tools and aids to help you communicate with your Shiba Inu and reinforce desired behaviors. In this chapter, we'll explore some of the most common training tools and aids that can enhance your training sessions.

Training Tools and Aids

Clicker

Purpose: Clickers are used for clicker training, a form of positive reinforcement. The distinct clicking sound marks the exact moment your Shiba Inu exhibits the desired behavior.

How to Use: Pair the clicker with treats or rewards. Click when your Shiba Inu performs the desired behavior, immediately followed by a treat. This clear signal helps your dog understand what behavior is being rewarded.

Treat Pouch

Purpose: A treat pouch is a convenient way to carry and dispense treats during training sessions. It keeps treats easily accessible, allowing for quick rewards.

How to Use: Attach the treat pouch to your waist or belt for easy access. Reward your Shiba Inu promptly after they exhibit the desired behavior.

Training Leash

Purpose: Training leashes come in various lengths and styles, designed for specific training goals. They provide control and safety during training sessions.

How to Use: Choose the appropriate training leash for your needs. Short leashes are ideal for heel and obedience training, while long lines are useful for recall training and teaching off-leash commands.

Harness

Purpose: A harness is an alternative to a collar and can provide better control, especially for dogs prone to pulling. It also distributes pressure more evenly across the body.

How to Use: Ensure the harness fits comfortably and securely. Attach the leash to the harness for added control during walks and training exercises.

Training Collar

Purpose: Training collars, such as martingale collars or slip collars, can be used for leash training and behavior correction. They provide a controlled and gentle way to guide your dog's movements.

How to Use: Ensure the collar is properly fitted and used according to the manufacturer's instructions. Avoid using excessive force or causing discomfort to your Shiba Inu.

Target Stick

Purpose: A target stick is a tool used in clicker training to guide your Shiba Inu's movements. It provides a visual target for your dog to follow.

How to Use: Present the target stick, and when your Shiba Inu touches it with their nose or paw, click and reward. This helps shape specific behaviors and positions.

Training Treat Dispensers

Purpose: Treat dispensers, like puzzle toys or automatic treat dispensing devices, provide mental stimulation during training and play.

How to Use: Load the dispenser with treats and let your Shiba Inu figure out how to access them. This engages their problem-solving skills and keeps them mentally stimulated.

Whistle

Purpose: Whistles can be used for recall training and long-distance communication during off-leash activities.

How to Use: Pair the whistle with a specific recall command, such as "come." Train your Shiba Inu to associate the whistle sound with the command, rewarding them for a successful response.

Choosing the Right Tools

The choice of training tools and aids depends on your training goals and your Shiba Inu's individual needs. It's important to use these tools responsibly and humanely, always prioritizing your dog's comfort and safety. Additionally, consider consulting a professional dog trainer for guidance on selecting and using training tools effectively. With the right tools and positive reinforcement techniques, you can enjoy successful training sessions and strengthen the bond between you and your Shiba Inu.

Training Environment

Creating the right training environment is crucial for successful training sessions with your Shiba Inu. In this chapter, we'll explore the elements of an effective training place and how to optimize it for productive training.

The Importance of a Training Environment

A dedicated training environment provides structure, consistency, and focus for both you and your Shiba Inu. It helps eliminate distractions and enhances your ability to communicate and reinforce desired behaviors.

Elements of an Ideal Training Place

Quiet and Controlled: Choose a location that is quiet and free from excessive noise and distractions. A controlled environment allows you to maintain your Shiba Inu's attention and helps them concentrate on the training.

Safe and Secure: Safety is paramount during training. Ensure the area is secure, whether indoors or outdoors, to prevent your Shiba Inu from escaping or encountering potential hazards.

Well-Lit: A well-lit environment ensures visibility and clarity during training sessions. Adequate lighting helps both you and your Shiba Inu understand each other's cues and body language.

Free from Clutter: A clutter-free space minimizes distractions and trip hazards. Remove unnecessary objects and obstacles that could divert your Shiba Inu's attention or pose risks.

Limited Access: Control access to the training area. This helps prevent interruptions from other people or pets and maintains a focused training environment.

Comfortable Flooring: Choose a surface that is comfortable and safe for your Shiba Inu. Indoors, non-slip flooring can help prevent accidents. Outdoors, ensure the ground is free from sharp objects or potential irritants.

Adequate Space: Having enough space for training exercises is essential. Different commands and activities may require varying amounts of room. Ensure you have space for your Shiba Inu to move comfortably.

Optimizing Your Training Place

Consistency: Use the same training place whenever possible. Consistency helps your Shiba Inu associate the environment with training and focus.

Minimize Distractions: Remove or reduce distractions as much as possible. This might involve closing doors, using barriers, or training during quieter times of the day.

Use Visual Cues: Mark the training place with visual cues that signal training sessions. This helps your Shiba Inu understand when it's time to work and when it's time for other activities.

Adequate Supplies: Have all your training materials and tools ready before starting a session. This prevents interruptions and keeps the training flowing smoothly.

Positive Associations: Make the training place a positive and enjoyable space for your Shiba Inu. Use treats, praise, and toys to create positive associations with the training area.

Outdoor vs. Indoor Training

Both indoor and outdoor environments can be suitable for training, depending on your goals and your Shiba Inu's needs. Indoor spaces offer more control and fewer distractions, while outdoor areas provide exposure to real-world scenarios.

Toys and Their Role

Toys play a vital role in Shiba Inu training and overall well-being. In this chapter, we'll explore the significance of toys in training, the types of toys that best suit your Shiba Inu, and how to use them effectively during training sessions.

The Importance of Toys in Training

Motivation: Toys are excellent motivators for your Shiba Inu. They can be used as rewards during training sessions to reinforce good behavior. The promise of playtime with their favorite toy can encourage your Shiba Inu to perform commands correctly.

Mental Stimulation: Interactive toys challenge your Shiba Inu mentally. Engaging their problem-solving skills with toys like puzzle feeders or treat-dispensing toys keeps their mind sharp and prevents boredom.

Bonding: Playing with your Shiba Inu using toys can strengthen your bond. It's an opportunity for quality one-on-one time, building trust and a positive relationship.

Exercise: Certain toys, such as fetch toys or tug ropes, provide physical exercise for your Shiba Inu. Regular play sessions help them expend energy and maintain a healthy weight.

Choosing the Right Toys

Not all toys are suitable for Shiba Inus, so it's important to select toys that match their needs and preferences:

Durability: Shiba Inus are known for their strong jaws, so choose durable toys that can withstand chewing and play. Look for toys made of tough materials like rubber, nylon, or reinforced fabric.

Size: Select toys that are an appropriate size for your Shiba Inu. Avoid toys that are too small and could be a choking hazard, or toys that are too large and cumbersome for them to carry or play with comfortably.

Texture: Vary the textures of toys to keep your Shiba Inu engaged. Toys with different textures, such as ridges, bumps, and soft plush, can provide sensory stimulation.

Interactive Toys: Consider interactive toys that challenge your Shiba Inu's problem-solving abilities. Puzzle toys and treat-dispensing toys are excellent choices to provide mental stimulation.

Chew Toys: Chew toys can help satisfy your Shiba Inu's natural urge to chew while also promoting dental health. Look for toys designed to clean teeth and massage gums.

Fetch Toys: If your Shiba Inu enjoys fetch, invest in a suitable fetch toy. Balls, frisbees, and flying discs are popular options for active play.

Using Toys in Training

Here are some ways to effectively incorporate toys into your Shiba Inu's training:

Reward-Based Training: Use toys as rewards for good behavior during training sessions. After your Shiba Inu successfully follows a command, play a short game with their favorite toy as a positive reinforcement.

Distraction-Free Training: Before beginning training exercises, let your Shiba Inu burn off excess energy with a brief play session. This helps them focus better during training, as they're less likely to be distracted by pent-up energy.

Problem-Solving Exercises: Utilize puzzle toys to engage your Shiba Inu's problem-solving skills. These toys can be used for commands like "find it" or to encourage exploration and curiosity.

Obedience Training: Incorporate toys into obedience training exercises, such as using a fetch toy to practice "drop it" or "leave it" commands.

Interactive Play: Interactive playtime with toys, like tug-of-war or fetch, can be a fun way to reinforce training and exercise at the same time.

Safety Considerations

Always prioritize your Shiba Inu's safety when using toys in training:

- Regularly inspect toys for signs of wear and replace damaged toys to prevent choking hazards.

- Supervise playtime to ensure your Shiba Inu doesn't ingest or destroy toys.

- Avoid toys with small parts that could be swallowed.

- Be cautious with tug-of-war games to prevent injury to your Shiba Inu's teeth or jaw.

Toys are valuable tools in Shiba Inu training that provide motivation, mental stimulation, and opportunities for bonding. By selecting the right toys for your Shiba Inu and incorporating them into your training routine, you can enhance the learning experience and create a happy, engaged, and well-behaved companion. Remember to prioritize safety and monitor playtime to ensure your Shiba Inu enjoys the benefits of toys while staying safe and healthy.

Crate Training

Crate training is a valuable tool in raising a well-behaved and comfortable Shiba Inu. In this chapter, we'll explore the benefits of crate training, how to introduce your Shiba Inu to their crate, and the steps to successful crate training.

The Benefits of Crate Training

Safe Space: A crate provides a secure and designated space for your Shiba Inu, offering a sense of safety and comfort.

Housetraining Aid: Crate training aids in housetraining by encouraging your Shiba Inu to hold their bladder and bowels until they can be taken outside.

Preventing Destructive Behavior: When unsupervised, Shiba Inus can engage in destructive behavior. A crate keeps them contained and prevents damage to your home.

Travel and Vet Visits: Crate-trained Shiba Inus are more comfortable during travel and vet visits, as they are accustomed to being in confined spaces.

Managing Separation Anxiety: For some Shiba Inus, a crate can provide a sense of security when left alone, helping to manage separation anxiety.

Emergency Situations: In case of emergencies, a crate-trained Shiba Inu is easier to manage and evacuate safely.

Introducing Your Shiba Inu to Their Crate

Proper introduction to the crate is essential to ensure your Shiba Inu views it as a positive and safe space:

Choose the Right Crate: Select an appropriately sized crate. It should be large enough for your Shiba Inu to stand up, turn around, and lie down comfortably, but not so large that they can eliminate in one corner and sleep in another.

Make It Inviting: Place a comfortable bedding or blanket inside the crate to make it inviting. Add a few toys or chew items to keep your Shiba Inu occupied.

Familiarization: Allow your Shiba Inu to explore the crate at their own pace. Leave the door open and encourage them to enter with treats or toys. Do not force them inside.

Positive Associations: Associate the crate with positive experiences. Feed your Shiba Inu their meals near the crate, gradually moving the food bowl inside.

Short Intervals: Start with short intervals of crating while you are present. Praise and reward your Shiba Inu when they enter the crate willingly.

Gradual Alone Time: As your Shiba Inu becomes comfortable with the crate, start leaving them in it for short periods while you are nearby. Gradually increase the duration as they become more at ease.

Avoid Punishment: Never use the crate as a form of punishment. It should remain a positive and secure space for your Shiba Inu.

Crate Training Steps

Once your Shiba Inu is accustomed to the crate, follow these steps for successful crate training:

Feeding in the Crate: Continue to feed your Shiba Inu their meals inside the crate. This reinforces the positive association with the crate.

Crate as a Resting Place: Encourage your Shiba Inu to use the crate for rest and relaxation voluntarily. Place a soft bed or blanket inside for comfort.

Gradual Alone Time: Begin leaving your Shiba Inu in the crate for short periods when you need to leave the house. Use treats or toys to keep them occupied.

Housetraining: During housetraining, use the crate to prevent accidents when you cannot supervise your Shiba Inu. Take them outside immediately after releasing them from the crate.

Gradual Freedom: Over time, gradually increase the freedom your Shiba Inu has in the house. Monitor their behavior, and if they demonstrate reliability, you can allow them more freedom.

Nighttime Crating: For nighttime, place the crate in your bedroom initially to comfort your Shiba Inu. As they become more comfortable, you can move it to a preferred location.

Common Crate Training Mistakes to Avoid

Using the crate for excessive periods: Avoid leaving your Shiba Inu crated for extended periods. They need social interaction and exercise.

Not making it positive: The crate should always be associated with positive experiences, not punishment.

Ignoring vocalizations: If your Shiba Inu whines or barks in the crate, address their needs promptly, but do not release them until they are calm.

Inconsistent use: Be consistent with crate training. Inconsistency can confuse your Shiba Inu.

Crate training is a valuable tool for Shiba Inu owners, providing numerous benefits for both your dog and your household. With patience, positive reinforcement, and gradual acclimation, you can successfully crate train your Shiba Inu and create a safe and comfortable space for them to enjoy.

Commands

Commands

Chapter Four

Basic Commands

Basic commands are the building blocks of obedience and communication between you and your Shiba Inu. In this chapter, we'll explore essential commands like "Sit," "Stay," "Come," "Drop it," "Fetch," "Down," and "Name Recognition." These commands form the foundation for a well-behaved and responsive Shiba Inu.

Sit

Purpose: The "Sit" command is one of the first commands you should teach your Shiba Inu. It promotes calmness and control, especially during greetings or when attaching the leash.

How to Teach: Hold a treat above your Shiba Inu's head and move it back over their eyes. As they follow the treat, their bottom will naturally lower to the ground. Say "Sit" as they do so, and reward them.

Stay

Purpose: "Stay" is vital for keeping your Shiba Inu safe and well-behaved. It prevents them from running into dangerous situations or wandering off.

How to Teach: Begin with your Shiba Inu in a sitting position. Hold your hand, palm out, in front of their face and say "Stay." Step back a short distance. If they stay in place, reward them. Gradually increase the distance and duration.

Come (Recall)

Purpose: The "Come" or "Here" command is crucial for calling your Shiba Inu back to you, whether during play, walks, or off-leash activities.

How to Teach: Use a cheerful tone and say "Come" while crouching down or kneeling. Encourage your Shiba Inu to come to you with open arms and excitement. When they reach you, reward them generously.

Drop it

Purpose: "Drop it" teaches your Shiba Inu to release items they have picked up, which is essential for their safety and preventing them from chewing on or swallowing harmful objects.

How to Teach: Begin by offering a toy to your Shiba Inu. When they take it, say "Drop it" and present a more enticing treat. As they drop the toy for the treat, reward them and praise their choice.

Fetch

Purpose: Fetch is a fun and engaging game that provides exercise and mental stimulation for your Shiba Inu.

How to Teach: Start with a favorite toy. Toss it a short distance and say "Fetch" as your Shiba Inu goes to retrieve it. When they bring the toy back, say "Drop it," as discussed earlier.

Down

Purpose: The "Down" command is used to make your Shiba Inu lie down, which can be useful in various situations, including calming them down.

How to Teach: Begin with your Shiba Inu in a sitting position. Hold a treat near their nose, then slowly move it down to the ground. Say "Down" as they follow the treat with their nose and lower themselves. Reward them when they are in a down position.

Name Recognition

Purpose: Teaching your Shiba Inu to respond to their name is the first step in effective communication. It helps gain their attention and focus.

How to Teach: Say your Shiba Inu's name in a cheerful tone. When they look at you, reward them with praise and a treat. Repeat this often, gradually increasing the distance between you and your Shiba Inu.

Training Tips:

Short Sessions: Keep training sessions short and positive to prevent frustration for both you and your Shiba Inu.

Consistency: Be consistent with your commands and rewards. Use the same cues and praise each time.

Positive Reinforcement: Always use positive reinforcement, such as treats, praise, and affection, to reward desired behaviors.

Patience: Practice patience and understanding during training. Every dog learns at their own pace.

Practice in Different Environments: Gradually practice these commands in various settings to ensure your Shiba Inu can respond reliably in different situations.

By mastering these basic commands, you'll establish a strong foundation for further training and ensure that your Shiba Inu is well-behaved, responsive, and a joy to be around.

Advanced Commands

Once you've established a strong foundation with basic commands, it's time to take your Shiba Inu's training to the next level with advanced commands. These commands not only challenge their cognitive abilities but also strengthen the bond between you and your furry companion. In this chapter, we'll explore advanced commands.

Heel

Purpose: The "Heel" command teaches your Shiba Inu to walk politely by your side without pulling on the leash, making walks more enjoyable and controlled.

How to Teach: Start with your Shiba Inu on a leash. Hold treats by your side, and use the command "Heel." Encourage them to walk beside you. Reward them generously when they do so.

Leave it

Purpose: "Leave it" is a crucial command to prevent your Shiba Inu from picking up or showing interest in potentially dangerous or undesirable items.

How to Teach: Offer your Shiba Inu a treat in a closed fist. When they try to investigate, say "Leave it." Wait for them to stop showing interest, then open your hand and reward them with a different treat.

Wait

Purpose: "Wait" teaches your Shiba Inu to pause and stay in one place until given further instructions, which is useful in various situations.

How to Teach: Use the "Wait" command while your Shiba Inu is on a leash or in a controlled environment. Ask them to sit or stand and say "Wait." Then, take a step back. If they remain in place, reward them.

Shake Hands

Purpose: "Shake Hands" is a charming and friendly command that allows your Shiba Inu to greet people politely.

How to Teach: Offer your hand and say "Shake" or "Paw." Gently lift your Shiba Inu's paw and shake it. Reward them with a treat and praise. Practice until they can do it without your assistance.

High Five

Purpose: Similar to shaking hands, "High Five" adds a playful twist to the command and can be a fun trick to show off.

How to Teach: Hold your hand up and say "High Five" or "Give me five." Encourage your Shiba Inu to touch your hand with their paw. Reward and praise them when they do.

Roll Over

Purpose: "Roll Over" is a playful command that demonstrates your Shiba Inu's obedience and agility.

How to Teach: Begin with your Shiba Inu in a down position. Hold a treat near their nose and move it around their head, saying "Roll Over" as they follow the treat and roll onto their back. Reward and praise them.

Crawl

Purpose: "Crawl" is a fun command that challenges your Shiba Inu to move forward while staying low to the ground.

How to Teach: Start with your Shiba Inu in a down position. Hold a treat in front of them and say "Crawl." Encourage them to move forward while keeping their belly close to the ground. Reward their progress.

Weave

Purpose: "Weave" is an advanced agility command that involves your Shiba Inu navigating a series of obstacles or your legs while walking.

How to Teach: Use a series of objects or your legs as obstacles. Begin by walking slowly and saying "Weave." Guide your Shiba Inu through the obstacles, rewarding them at the end.

Play Dead

Purpose: "Play Dead" is a fun and impressive trick that showcases your Shiba Inu's training and intelligence.

How to Teach: Start with your Shiba Inu in a down position. Hold a treat near their nose and say "Play Dead." Gently guide them onto their side. Reward them for holding the position.

Training Tips:

Consistency: Be consistent with your commands and rewards to reinforce the desired behavior.

Short Sessions: Keep training sessions short and positive to maintain your Shiba Inu's enthusiasm.

Patience: Advanced commands may take more time to master, so practice patience and provide plenty of encouragement.

Positive Reinforcement: Always use positive reinforcement, such as treats, praise, and affection, to reward successful execution of advanced commands.

Practice: Regular practice is essential for maintaining proficiency in advanced commands.

Clicker Training

Clicker training is a highly effective and positive reinforcement-based method for teaching your Shiba Inu new behaviors and commands. In this chapter, we'll explore the principles of clicker training, how to get started, and its benefits in shaping your Shiba Inu's behavior.

What is Clicker Training?

Clicker training is a training method that uses a small handheld device called a clicker to mark the precise moment your Shiba Inu exhibits a desired behavior. The clicker emits a distinct clicking sound that signals to your dog that they've done something right, followed by a reward (usually a treat).

How Clicker Training Works:

Mark the Behavior: When your Shiba Inu performs the desired behavior, click the clicker immediately. The click serves as a clear and consistent marker.

Reward: After clicking, immediately reward your dog with a treat or other positive reinforcement. This reinforces the connection between the click and the reward.

Repeat: Continue to practice and reinforce the behavior with the clicker and rewards. Over time, your Shiba Inu will associate the click with the correct action.

Benefits of Clicker Training

Clicker training offers several advantages for training your Shiba Inu:

Precision: Clicker training allows for precise timing, making it easy to pinpoint the exact moment your Shiba Inu exhibits the desired behavior. This clarity helps your dog understand what they're being rewarded for.

Positive Reinforcement: Clicker training relies on positive reinforcement, which is a humane and effective method. Your Shiba Inu associates the click with a reward, motivating them to repeat the desired behavior.

Communication: The clicker serves as a consistent form of communication between you and your Shiba Inu. It eliminates the need for verbal cues, which can sometimes be confusing or inconsistent.

Mental Stimulation: Clicker training engages your Shiba Inu's mental faculties as they actively try to figure out which behavior earns them the click and subsequent reward. This mental stimulation can prevent boredom and promote a healthy, active mind.

Bonding: Clicker training fosters a strong bond between you and your Shiba Inu. It's a collaborative and rewarding experience that enhances your relationship.

Getting Started with Clicker Training

Follow these steps to begin clicker training your Shiba Inu:

Acquire a Clicker: Purchase a clicker designed for dog training. They are readily available at pet stores and online. Ensure the clicker is easy to use and comfortable to hold.

Charge the Clicker: Before using the clicker with your Shiba Inu, "charge" it by clicking and immediately rewarding your dog with a treat multiple times in a row. This helps them associate the click with a positive outcome.

Start with Basic Behaviors: Begin with basic behaviors your Shiba Inu already knows, such as "Sit" or "Stay." Click and reward when they perform the behavior correctly. Gradually introduce the clicker to new behaviors.

Be Consistent: Consistency is key in clicker training. Click and reward every time your Shiba Inu exhibits the desired behavior. This reinforcement strengthens their understanding of the command.

Keep Sessions Short: Clicker training sessions should be short and focused, typically lasting around 5-10 minutes. This prevents frustration and maintains your Shiba Inu's interest.

Gradually Fade the Clicker: As your Shiba Inu becomes proficient in responding to the clicker, you can gradually reduce its use. Click less frequently and rely more on verbal cues and rewards.

Common Clicker Training Mistakes to Avoid:

Inconsistent Timing: Click at the precise moment your Shiba Inu performs the desired behavior. Inconsistent timing can lead to confusion.

Skipping Rewards: Always follow the click with a reward. Skipping rewards can reduce the effectiveness of the clicker.

Overloading with Information: Avoid overwhelming your Shiba Inu with too many new behaviors at once. Focus on one behavior at a time.

Ignoring Individual Preferences: Tailor your choice of treats to your Shiba Inu's preferences. Use high-value treats that they find especially enticing.

Clicker training is a rewarding and effective method for teaching your Shiba Inu new behaviors and commands while strengthening your bond. With patience, consistency, and positive reinforcement, you can use the clicker to communicate and collaborate with your Shiba Inu, leading to a well-behaved and happy companion.

Walks & Adventures

Walks are an essential part of a Shiba Inu's routine, providing exercise, mental stimulation, and opportunities for bonding. In this chapter, we'll explore the importance of walks, leash training, safety considerations, and tips for enjoyable walks with your Shiba Inu.

The Importance of Walks

Exercise: Walks provide essential physical activity, helping your Shiba Inu maintain a healthy weight and preventing obesity.

Mental Stimulation: Exploring new scents, sights, and sounds during walks stimulates your Shiba Inu's mind and prevents boredom.

Socialization: Walks allow your Shiba Inu to encounter other dogs, people, and various environments, promoting positive socialization.

Bonding: Walking together strengthens the bond between you and your Shiba Inu, enhancing your relationship.

Leash Training

Start Early: Begin leash training when your Shiba Inu is a puppy to establish good habits from the start.

Choose the Right Leash: Select a comfortable, sturdy leash that suits your Shiba Inu's size and strength.

Use Positive Reinforcement: Reward your Shiba Inu for walking nicely on a leash. Offer treats and praise when they walk without pulling.

Practice Patience: Be patient during leash training. If your Shiba Inu pulls, stop walking and wait until they relax the tension on the leash before continuing.

Vary Your Routes: Explore different routes and environments during walks to keep your Shiba Inu engaged and mentally stimulated.

Safety Considerations

Proper Identification: Always have an ID tag with your contact information on your Shiba Inu's collar. Consider microchipping as an added precaution.

Leash Control: Maintain control of the leash at all times to prevent your Shiba Inu from bolting or getting into unsafe situations.

Traffic and Hazards: Be cautious near roads and traffic. Watch for potential hazards like broken glass or toxic substances.

Weather Conditions: Adjust the duration and intensity of walks based on weather conditions. Protect your Shiba Inu from extreme heat or cold.

Parasite Prevention: Ensure your Shiba Inu is protected against fleas, ticks, and heartworms, which can be encountered during outdoor activities.

Tips for Enjoyable Walks

Exploration: Allow your Shiba Inu to explore and sniff their surroundings. It's mentally stimulating and satisfying for them.

Positive Reinforcement: Use treats, praise, and affection as rewards during walks to reinforce good behavior.

Variety: Change your walking routes to keep things interesting for your Shiba Inu. Visit parks, trails, and new neighborhoods.

Pack Essentials: Bring essentials like waste bags, water, and a collapsible bowl for longer walks.

Be Attentive: Pay attention to your Shiba Inu's body language. If they appear anxious or uncomfortable, be prepared to address their needs.

Socialization: Use walks as an opportunity for positive socialization with other dogs and people. Ensure your Shiba Inu is well-behaved around others.

Canine Sports and Activities

Engaging in canine sports and activities is an excellent way to keep your Shiba Inu physically fit, mentally stimulated, and emotionally satisfied. In this chapter, we'll explore various canine sports and activities, including Agility, Jogging, Flyball, Herding, Soccer, Rally Obedience, Dog Dancing, and Swimming, that you can enjoy with your Shiba Inu.

Agility

Purpose: Agility is a fast-paced sport that involves your Shiba Inu navigating a timed obstacle course, including jumps, tunnels, weave poles, and more.

Benefits: Agility enhances your Shiba Inu's agility, balance, and coordination while providing mental stimulation. It fosters a strong bond between you and your dog through teamwork.

Jogging

Purpose: Jogging or running with your Shiba Inu is an excellent way to provide cardiovascular exercise and expend energy.

Benefits: Regular jogging helps maintain your Shiba Inu's physical fitness and can improve their endurance. It also offers a chance for you both to explore new places together.

Flyball

Purpose: Flyball is a relay race for dogs, where they jump over hurdles, trigger a spring-loaded box to release a tennis ball, and then return with the ball.

Benefits: This high-energy sport builds speed and agility in your Shiba Inu while promoting teamwork and coordination. It's a fun and competitive activity.

Soccer

Purpose: Playing soccer with your Shiba Inu involves dribbling, passing, and scoring goals with a soccer ball.

Benefits: Soccer is a fun way to improve your Shiba Inu's coordination, agility, and stamina. It provides an outlet for their energy and promotes bonding.

Swimming

Purpose: Swimming is a low-impact exercise that helps keep your Shiba Inu fit and cool, especially during hot weather.

Benefits: Swimming is gentle on the joints and muscles while providing an excellent cardiovascular workout. It's also a valuable skill for water safety.

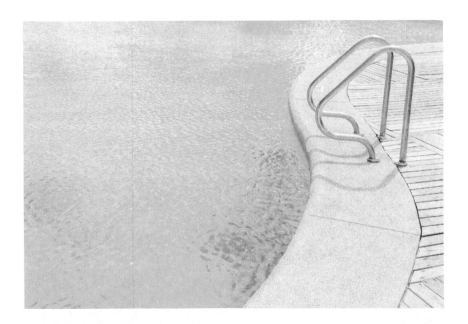

Rally Obedience

Purpose: Rally Obedience is a competitive sport that combines elements of obedience and agility. Your Shiba Inu follows a course of signs with various commands.

Benefits: Rally Obedience enhances obedience and responsiveness. It's a great way to reinforce basic commands and improve your dog's focus.

Dog Dancing

Purpose: Dog dancing, or canine freestyle, involves choreographing routines set to music, with your Shiba Inu performing a variety of tricks and moves.

Benefits: This creative sport promotes bonding, mental stimulation, and physical coordination. It's an excellent outlet for showcasing your Shiba Inu's skills.

Herding (Treibball)

Purpose: Herding or Treibball is a sport where dogs use their herding instincts to move large exercise balls into a goal, simulating herding livestock.

Benefits: Herding activities satisfy your Shiba Inu's natural herding instincts while challenging their problem-solving skills and obedience.

Getting Started with Canine Sports

Consult Your Vet: Before starting any new sport or activity, consult your veterinarian to ensure your Shiba Inu is physically fit and healthy.

Training: Ensure your Shiba Inu has basic obedience training and recalls well before participating in any sport.

Safety: Always prioritize safety by using appropriate gear, such as harnesses, leashes, or safety equipment required for specific sports.

Start Slow: Introduce new activities gradually and at your Shiba Inu's pace. Overexertion can lead to injury or exhaustion.

Positive Reinforcement: Use positive reinforcement, treats, and praise to encourage participation and good behavior during sports.

Have Fun: Most importantly, enjoy the experience with your Shiba Inu. Canine sports and activities are not only beneficial but also a source of joy and companionship.

By exploring and participating in these canine sports and activities, you can keep your Shiba Inu physically and mentally engaged while strengthening your bond through shared experiences and fun-filled adventures.

Mental Stimulation & Brain Games

Mental stimulation and brain games are essential for keeping your Shiba Inu's active mind engaged and preventing boredom. In this chapter, we'll explore the importance of mental stimulation, various types of brain games, and how to incorporate them into your Shiba Inu's daily routine.

The Importance of Mental Stimulation

Prevents Boredom: A bored Shiba Inu may resort to destructive behaviors. Mental stimulation keeps their minds occupied and content.

Promotes Problem-Solving: Brain games challenge your Shiba Inu to think and problem-solve, which can improve their cognitive abilities.

Strengthens Bond: Engaging in activities together fosters a stronger bond between you and your Shiba Inu.

Reduces Anxiety: Mental stimulation can help alleviate anxiety and restlessness in your dog.

Types of Brain Games

Puzzle Toys: Puzzle toys are designed to dispense treats or kibble when your Shiba Inu figures out how to manipulate the toy. Examples include treat-dispensing balls, puzzle feeders, and interactive toys.

Hide and Seek: Hide treats or toys around your home and encourage your Shiba Inu to find them. Start with easy hiding spots and gradually increase the difficulty.

Scent Games: Hide a treat or favorite toy in a room and allow your Shiba Inu to use their keen sense of smell to locate it. You can also use scent trails or scent-detection games.

Interactive Feeding Toys

Instead of using a regular food bowl, feed your Shiba Inu with interactive feeding toys like slow-feeders or snuffle mats. These require your dog to work for their food.

Training and Obedience Drills: Regular training sessions provide mental stimulation. Teach your Shiba Inu new tricks or reinforce existing commands.

Rotate Toys: Keep a variety of toys available and rotate them regularly. Novelty keeps your Shiba Inu engaged and curious.

DIY Brain Games: Create your own brain games, such as homemade treat puzzles or cardboard box challenges. Be creative and tailor them to your Shiba Inu's preferences.

Incorporating Brain Games into Daily Routine

Here's how to integrate mental stimulation and brain games into your Shiba Inu's daily routine:

Scheduled Playtime: Allocate specific times each day for interactive play and brain games.

Training Sessions: Incorporate short training sessions into your daily routine, focusing on commands, tricks, or new skills.

Mealtime Challenge: Use interactive feeders or puzzle toys to make mealtime more engaging.

Outdoor Exploration: During walks, allow your Shiba Inu to explore and use their senses. Change routes and environments to keep things interesting.

Rotate Toys: Keep a selection of toys available and rotate them to maintain novelty.

Social Interaction: Arrange playdates with other dogs to provide social and mental stimulation.

Challenge Their Senses: Set up sensory stations with different textures, objects, and smells for your Shiba Inu to investigate.

Quality Time: Spend quality time together, whether it's through training, play, or just relaxing together.

Benefits of Mental Stimulation

Engaging in brain games and mental stimulation offers several benefits:

Prevents Destructive Behavior: Mental stimulation reduces the likelihood of your Shiba Inu engaging in destructive behaviors out of boredom.

Enhances Cognitive Skills: These activities improve problem-solving abilities and overall cognitive function.

Reduces Anxiety: Mental stimulation can help alleviate anxiety and restlessness in your Shiba Inu.

Strengthens Bond: Sharing brain games and activities strengthens your bond and deepens your relationship.

Promotes a Happy and Healthy Dog: A mentally stimulated Shiba Inu is a content and well-adjusted dog.

By incorporating brain games and mental stimulation into your Shiba Inu's daily routine, you'll provide them with the intellectual challenges they crave and ensure their overall happiness and well-being.

Puppy Classes, Dog Schools, and Trainers

Ensuring your Shiba Inu receives proper training and socialization is essential for their development and well-being. In this chapter, we'll explore the benefits of enrolling your Shiba Inu in puppy classes, dog schools, and the role of professional trainers in their upbringing.

The Importance of Proper Training

Proper training is crucial for Shiba Inu puppies to become well-adjusted, obedient, and socially adept adults. Here's why it matters:

Socialization: Puppy classes and dog schools provide opportunities for early socialization with other dogs and people, reducing the likelihood of fear or aggression issues in adulthood.

Basic Obedience: Training teaches essential commands like "Sit," "Stay," and "Come," ensuring your Shiba Inu's safety and your peace of mind.

Behavioral Management: Professional trainers can address and manage unwanted behaviors, preventing them from becoming long-term problems.

Bonding: Training strengthens the bond between you and your Shiba Inu, fostering trust and cooperation.

Mental Stimulation: Training challenges your Shiba Inu mentally, keeping their active minds engaged and satisfied.

Puppy Classes

Puppy classes are typically group training sessions designed for puppies aged 8 to 16 weeks. Here's what you can expect:

Socialization: Puppies learn to interact with other dogs and people in a controlled and supervised environment.

Basic Commands: They are introduced to basic commands like "Sit," "Stay," and "Come."

Problem-Solving: Puppies engage in problem-solving activities that boost their cognitive abilities.

Behavior Management: Common puppy behaviors like biting, chewing, and housebreaking are addressed.

Positive Reinforcement: Puppy classes primarily use positive reinforcement techniques, creating a positive learning experience.

Dog Schools

Dog schools or obedience classes are ideal for puppies older than 4 months and adult Shiba Inus. Here's what you can expect from dog schools:

Structured Training: These classes offer a more structured approach to training, covering a range of commands and behaviors.

Distraction Training: Dogs learn to obey commands amidst various distractions, preparing them for real-world situations.

Behavior Modification: Classes address specific behavioral issues, such as aggression or anxiety.

Advanced Training: Beyond basic obedience, dog schools offer advanced training for more complex commands and activities.

Professional Guidance: Instructors at dog schools are experienced trainers who can provide expert guidance.

Professional Trainers

Professional trainers can be valuable resources for Shiba Inu owners. Here's how they can assist:

Customized Training: Trainers can create customized training plans tailored to your Shiba Inu's specific needs and challenges.

Behavior Modification: They can address and modify problematic behaviors, such as aggression, separation anxiety, or excessive barking.

One-on-One Sessions: Personalized training sessions allow for focused attention and rapid progress.

Advanced Training: Professional trainers can guide your Shiba Inu through advanced obedience or specialized activities like agility or therapy work.

Continued Support: Trainers provide ongoing support and advice for long-term success.

How to Choose the Right Trainer or School

When selecting a trainer or school for your Shiba Inu, consider the following:

Reputation: Seek recommendations from trusted sources and read reviews to gauge the trainer's or school's reputation.

Certifications: Look for trainers with recognized certifications from organizations like the Association of Professional Dog Trainers (APDT) or the International Association of Canine Professionals (IACP).

Methods: Ensure the trainer uses positive reinforcement-based training methods, which are most effective and humane.

Experience: Inquire about the trainer's experience, especially with Shiba Inus or breeds with similar temperaments.

Compatibility: Choose a trainer or school that aligns with your training goals and philosophy.

Disclaimer:

The information and advice presented in this book are solely for informational purposes. The author and the publisher assume no responsibility for any losses or damages that may arise from the application of the information presented in this book. It is the responsibility of the reader to independently assess and determine whether the content and recommendations presented are suitable for their individual situation. Neither the author nor the publisher are liable for any errors or omissions in this book.

Copyright Disclaimer:

Imprint:

Christian Taormina
Kuchhauser Höhe 2
42349 Wuppertal